Floral Stencil Designs

Charlene Tarbox

Dover Publications, Inc., New York

To my parents, for their interest and encouragement

PUBLISHER'S NOTE

Floral designs are among the most in demand by decorators, artists and hobbyists. This all-new collection of original designs by Charlene Tarbox includes blossoms large and small, from the rose and the daisy, through the tulip, the daffodil and the lily, to the iris and the orchid. They appear singly, in sprays, gracefully intertwined, arranged as repeating motifs to form borders and other shapes, and within circular, rectangular and heart-shaped frames. The scope is broad enough to provide a stenciled floral image to suit every purpose.

Charlene Tarbox is a New York City painter, illustrator, fabric designer, teacher and author of *Floral Designs and Motifs for Artists, Needleworkers and Craftspeople* (Dover, 24716-3). She has found "the infinite variety of floral subjects as well as their historical treatment to be a constant source of inspiration."

Copyright © 1986 by Dover Publications, Inc.
All rights reserved under Pan American and International Copyright Conventions.

Published in Canada by General Publishing Company, Ltd., 30 Lesmill Road, Don Mills, Toronto, Ontario.

Published in the United Kingdom by Constable and Company, Ltd., 10 Orange Street, London WC2H 7EG.

Floral Stencil Designs is a new work, first published by Dover Publications, Inc., in 1986.

DOVER *Pictorial Archive* SERIES

Manufactured in the United States of America
Dover Publications, Inc., 31 East 2nd Street, Mineola, N.Y. 11501

Library of Congress Cataloging-in-Publication Data

Tarbox, Charlene.
  Floral stencil designs.
  (Dover pictorial archive series)
  1. Stencil work. 2. Decoration and ornament—Plant forms. I. Title. II. Series.
NK8655.T37   1986   745.7'3'0222   86-9011
  ISBN 0-486-25178-0

1

2

8

9

10

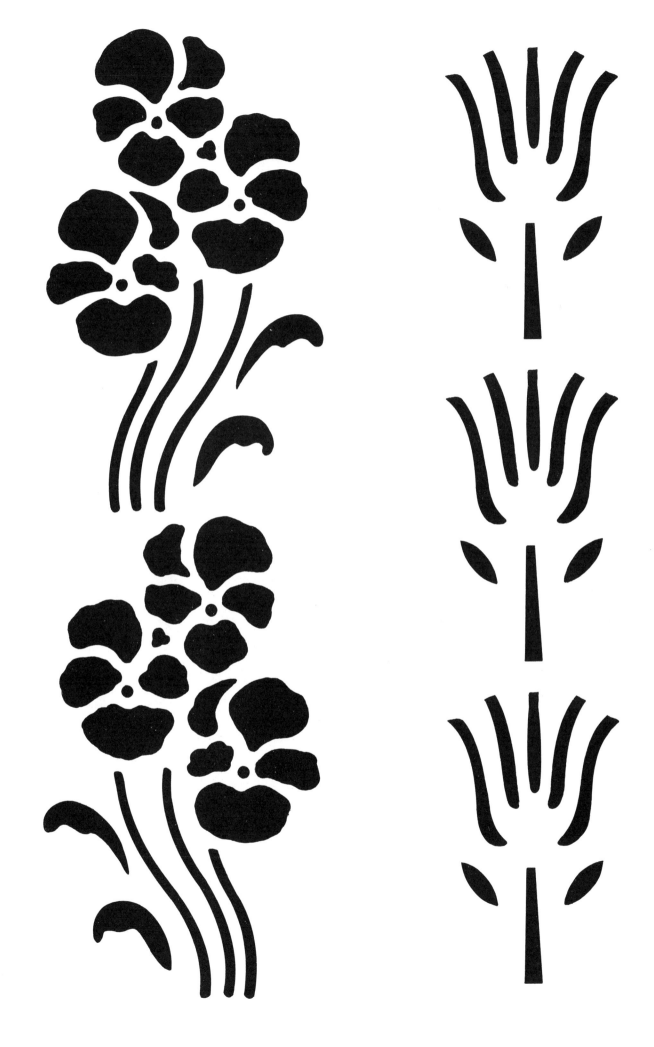

16

23

24

26

27

29

31

36

38

44

46

52

61

72